real thai

real thai

FROM CHICKEN AND LEMON GRASS CURRY TO SPICY MANGO SALAD

TERRY TAN

with photography by Peter Cassidy

jacqui
small

First published in 2007 by Jacqui Small,
an imprint of Aurum Press,
25 Bedford Avenue, London WC1B 3AT

Publisher   Jacqui Small
Editorial manager Kate John
Art Director   Ashley Western
Photographer   Peter Cassidy
Editor   Nicola Graimes
Props stylist   Roisin Nield
Production   Peter Colley

ISBN: 978 1 903221 66 2

2009 2008 2007

10 9 8 7 6 5 4 3 2 1

Printed in China

The recipes use both metric and imperial
measurements. Follow the same units of
measurement throughout – do not mix the two.
All spoon measurements are level: teaspoons are
5ml; and tablespoons are 15ml. Unless otherwise
stated, eggs, vegetables and fruits are assumed
to be medium in size.

Title page, from left: Seafood Green Curry, page 30; Grilled
Chicken in Coriander Sauce, page 34; Mango Salad, page 16;
and Tenderstem Broccoli with Oyster Sauce and Mushrooms,
page 44.

CONTENTS

INTRODUCTION

I have embraced Thai cuisine to my bosom growing up in a family where my paternal and maternal antecedents were an eclectic mix of Indonesian, Chinese and Thai. My father was Indonesian-Chinese, and my maternal grandmother was a fascinating hybrid of Thai, Chinese and Malay. Many of my maternal relatives hailed from southern Thailand and I learned much from osmosis.

My earliest memories are of particularly glorious weekends when inevitably I had the pungent task of grinding endless mortars of onions, chillies and eye-stinging pastes. These would go into curries redolent with spices, mouth-watering salads and numerous side dishes with their characteristic sharp, limey flavours and pungent aroma of fish sauce and shrimp pastes.

Whether searing hot or subtly aromatic, the principle in Thai cooking is harmony and balance. The cuisine has its origins in a waterborne lifestyle and aquatic animals, plants and herbs all play important roles. The cuisine has its soul in the rural heart of the country and it is not difficult to master the semantics of balance, the compatibility of ingredients and the many subtleties that underscore each dish.

The Thai Kitchen

In traditional Thai homes, whether rich or poor, the kitchen was almost always a separate part of the main house for a very good reason. Wood was always the main fuel and kitchens were smoky and stifling in the tropical heat and humidity. Many rural areas of Thailand still cook as they did centuries ago with wood and charcoal, though portable gas burners are making heated inroads. One of the earliest Thai stoves was an earthenware tray with one side raised to hold the bottom of a cooking pot and charcoal or wood embers placed under the pot. This was called a *cherng kran* and all but impossible to find these days. Today, more commonly used are built-in ranges made of tiled cement or terracotta. The more urban homes have portable gas rings, hobs or electric stoves much like those used in the west.

What now constitutes an adequately equipped kitchen is a wok, a few metal or earthenware pots, a steamer, either of aluminium or woven bamboo, a granite or terracotta pestle and mortar, various tools for scraping and processing such as coconuts and root vegetables, various baskets of woven pandanus for storage and service, a cleaver, a sharp paring knife and a chopping block. Of course, in affluent homes today, there are also a range of high tech implements like grinders, processors, and such like, to make short work of food processing.

Table Culture

It is often assumed that Thai's use chopsticks as often as the Chinese. In truth, the Thai dining table rarely features them and a typical place setting would be a large dinner plate, fork and spoon and perhaps a side bowl and porcelain spoon for soup. Chopsticks are employed only when soupy noodles are served. Every meal is communal wherein all the dishes are served at the same time and diners help themselves to each plate or bowl of curry, stir fried dishes, noodles or rice and side dips. In many rural pockets, Thais still eat with their fingers, using various leaves and rice crackers as makeshift spoons.

The Thai Store Cupboard

Many of the ingredients used in Thai cooking are now well known, however, there are still some that are not so familiar. The list overleaf gives you a brief description of some of the typical Thai ingredients used in this book.

Terry Tan

TERRY TAN

Spiced Chicken in Toei Leaves (page 18)

AUBERGINE (MAKREUA)

Thai aubergines (eggplant) come in all guises, ranging from tiny pea-sized ones to large, long, green, yellow or purple varieties. They impart a slightly nutty flavour when cooked.

BANANA LEAVES (BAI TONG)

The original throwaway plate, banana leaves impart a subtle perfume when used to wrap food. First blanch the leaves in boiling water to make them pliable and trim the hard spine before using as a wrapper.

BASIL (HORAPA)

There are three distinct types of basil used in Thai cooking: holy basil (*bai krapao*), lemon basil (*bai manglak*) and sweet basil (*horapa*), which is the most familiar. Sweet basil has purple stalks with a slight aniseed and mint flavour.

CHILLIES (PRIK CHEE)

The cornerstone of Thai cooking, chillies come in a range of heat intensities, from the extremely fiery bird's eye chilli (prik ki nu) to the mild, large green variety. Dried chillies are used mainly in curry pastes.

DRIED SHRIMPS (GUNG HAENG)

Indispensable in every Thai kitchen, dried shrimps are soaked and ground into pastes or chopped and added to salad dressings to give a rich, smoky flavour. A handful of them makes a good seasoning for soups.

FISH SAUCE (NAM PLA)

Made from fermented fish or prawns (shrimp), fish sauce is a potent seasoning that is an important part of most Thai savoury dishes and dips.

GALANGAL (KHA)

A member of the rhizome family and similar to ginger, galangal is an indispensable ingredient in many Thai curries; remember a little goes a long way. It is also known as *Laos root* or *blue ginger*.

LESSER GINGER (KRACHAI)

This type of ginger is a pungent cousin of galangal and comes in finger length roots clustered in a bunch. It has a strong flavour and should be used judiciously.

LEMON GRASS (TAKRAI)

Similar in appearance to a thick blade of grass, lemon grass can be chopped, sliced or ground into curry pastes or used whole in soups, curries and stir fries. Only about 5cm (2in) of the root end is used and it adds a characteristic elusive, aromatic lemon tang to Thai cooking.

KAFFIR LIME LEAVES (MAKRUT)

Together with lemon grass and galangal, kaffir lime leaves form the Thai holy trinity. The leaf has a heady fragrance for which there is no substitute. It can be used whole or ground into curry pastes.

MORNING GLORY (PAK BUNG)

An aquatic plant with hollow stems and thin green leaves, morning glory is packed with nutrients and flavour. Morning glory is also known as water convolvulus, swamp cabbage and water spinach.

PALM SUGAR (NAM TAN PUK)

Available in a variety of shapes and textures, such as dark brown cylinders or in tubs, palm sugar is made either from the sap of coconut palms or sugar palms. The nearest substitutes are brown muscovado or demerara sugar.

SHRIMP PASTE (KAPI)

This incredibly pungent ingredient is integral to almost all Thai spice pastes. Shrimp paste ranges from pale pink to dark brown in colour and should always be toasted or grilled before use as part of a dip, paste or in a curry.

TAMARIND (MAKARM)

A companion ingredient to coconut milk, tamarind comes in concentrated form, in ready-to-use tubs or as a dried pod. It has an acidic flavour and is the equivalent of lemon juice as used in western cooking.

TOEI LEAF (BAI TOEI HOM)

A fragrant member of the mangrove pandanus plant and also called screwpine, toei leaf has many uses in Thai cooking: as a wrapper; to perfume desserts; or ground for its vaguely vanilla essence and green colouring.

POMELO (SOM O)

Rather like a large grapefruit but with a thicker skin, pomelo has either a white or pink flesh. Depending on the ripeness and variety, it can be extremely tart or sweet. The segments separate easily and are eaten as a salad ingredient as well as a dessert.

APPETIZERS, SOUPS AND SALADS

In Thailand, you do not have to look too hard to discover the innate Thai passion for snacking. This spills over deliciously into every Thai meal and manifests in a tongue-tingling range of sensuous appetizers, simple soups, fragrant salads and other enticing small bites.

1 Use a saucer or cardboard template, about 15cm (6in) in diameter, to mark out a circle on each banana leaf, then cut out.

2 Fold in one side of the banana leaf circle and turn in the corner. Secure with a thin toothpick.

3 Fold in the next two sides and turn in the corners. Secure with thin toothpicks.

4 Fold in the remaining side to make an open box with a flat base and tapered top. Secure with a thin toothpick.

SPICED STEAMED FISH IN BANANA LEAF

Usually served as a tongue-teasing appetizer, these fish cakes are a wondrous bundle of intoxicating flavours that could also form part of a main meal. They look impressive served in their banana leaf cups and can also be baked or barbecued.

1 Chop the fish meat then blend in a food processor for a few minutes to make a paste.

2 Grind the paste ingredients together using a pestle and mortar or coffee grinder until the texture of thick cream, then blend with the fish.

3 Transfer the mixture to a bowl and add the fish sauce, lime juice and sugar then stir well until combined.

4 Lightly beat the eggs and add to the mixture with the coconut milk.

5 Trim the hard rind off the banana leaves and blanch for 1 minute in boiling water to make them more pliable; drain well.

6 Shape the banana leaves to make 8 cups following the instructions, left. Place 2 tablespoons of the fish mixture in the centre of each banana leaf cup.

7 Put the parcels on a plate in a steamer and steam for 10 minutes. You may need to cook the parcels in batches.

8 Drizzle a little coconut cream over each fish cake and garnish with the kaffir lime leaves and chilli. Serve with the sliced cucumber.

CHEF'S TIP: If banana leaves are unavailable, place the fish mixture in lightly oiled ramekins, cover with foil and steam for 15 minutes. Mix together 2 tablespoons of yellow curry paste (see page 62) and use instead of the spice paste, if preferred.

MAKES 8
450g (1lb) white fish, such as cod or halibut
2 tbsp fish sauce
2 tbsp lime juice
1 tsp sugar
2 eggs
4 tbsp thick coconut milk
8 banana leaves, each about 25cm (10in) square
sliced cucumber, to serve

FOR THE PASTE:
1 tbsp grated fresh ginger
2 red chillies, deseeded if liked
1 tsp turmeric
1 onion
2 stalks lemon grass, 5cm (2in) root end, peeled
1 tbsp ground coriander
1 tsp shrimp paste

TO GARNISH:
4 tbsp coconut cream
2 kaffir lime leaves, shredded
1 red chilli, finely sliced

TOM KHA GAI
CHICKEN AND COCONUT SOUP

A savoury, less spicy cousin of *tom yam kung*, this soup features coconut milk which successfully tempers the heat of the chillies.

SERVES 4

2–3 red chillies, deseeded and sliced
400ml (1^2/$_3$ cups) water
400ml (1^2/$_3$ cups) coconut milk
2 stalks lemon grass, 5cm (2in) root end, peeled and bruised
4 slices galangal (*kha*)
2 tbsp fish sauce
1 tbsp palm sugar
4 kaffir lime leaves
220g (8oz) skinless chicken breast
Sprigs of fresh coriander (cilantro) and fresh Thai sweet basil, to garnish

1 Deseed and slice the chillies and combine with the water, coconut milk, lemon grass, galangal, fish sauce, palm sugar and kaffir lime leaves in a saucepan. Bring to the boil then reduce the heat and simmer for 10 minutes.

2 Strain the stock and discard the solids. Dice the chicken breast and add to the pan with the strained stock. Simmer for 10 minutes until the chicken is cooked through.

3 Serve in individual bowls garnished with fresh coriander (cilantro) and Thai basil.

TOM YAM KUNG
HOT AND SOUR SEAFOOD SOUP

This soup can be easily adapted to suit personal taste; add more or less of each ingredient to create a highly individual flavour. When served in a steamboat, banquet-style, this soup is known as *po theak*.

SERVES 4

1 tbsp dried shrimps
2 red chillies, each about 5cm (2in) long, chopped
2 tbsp tamarind paste
850ml (3^1/$_2$ cups) water
4 kaffir lime leaves
4 bird's eye chillies
2 tbsp fish sauce
2 tbsp lime juice
2 stalks lemon grass, 5cm (2in) root end, peeled
16 medium raw prawns (shrimp), shelled
4 field mushrooms, sliced
freshly ground black pepper
fresh coriander (cilantro) leaves, to garnish

1 Soak the dried shrimps in hot water for 15 minutes until softened. Drain the shrimps then pound with the red chillies using a pestle and mortar until a fine paste.

2 Put the shrimp and chilli paste, tamarind, water, kaffir lime leaves, bird's eye chillies, fish sauce and lime juice into a small saucepan and simmer for 10 minutes.

3 Remove the kaffir lime leaves and chillies. Lightly crush the lemon grass with the blade of a knife then add to the pan and simmer for 5 minutes.

4 Add the prawns (shrimp) and mushrooms, stir, and simmer for a further 3 minutes. Season with black pepper and garnish with fresh coriander (cilantro) leaves before serving.

CHEF'S TIP: For a special touch, add 4 scallops with the prawns and mushrooms in step 4.

MANGO SALAD

Shredded and tossed in lime juice and spices, Thai green mangoes make fragrant salads. Use regular, orange-fleshed mangoes as an alternative but make sure they are not too ripe.

SERVES 2

200g (7oz) skinless chicken breast
1 green mango, about 250g (9oz)
4 Cos (Romaine) lettuce leaves
1 tbsp lime juice
1 tbsp English mustard
1 tsp sugar
2 tbsp sesame oil
$\frac{1}{2}$ tsp freshly ground black pepper

1 Slice the chicken breast into thin strips. Poach the chicken in a little water for 8 minutes until cooked through then drain and leave to cool.

2 Peel and slice the mango into long, thin strips. Shred the Cos (Romaine) lettuce leaves and toss with the chicken and mango in a large salad bowl.

3 Mix together the lime juice, mustard, sugar, sesame oil and black pepper. Drizzle over the salad and toss lightly.

CHEF'S TIP: *Som tham* is a sister salad to green mango, but uses a special Thai green papaya (paw paw).

1 Grate the carrot and finely shred the Chinese cabbage and leek. Soak the vermicelli noodles in just boiled water and drain well when soft. Leave to cool.

2 Heat 2 tablespoons of oil in a wok or large frying pan and stir-fry the carrot, cabbage and leek for 2 minutes until slightly tender.

3 Pat the tofu dry using kitchen towels and add to the wok. Mash the tofu with a wok ladle and stir-fry vigorously for 1 minute. Add the roasted peanuts, vermicelli and the seasonings. Remove from the wok and leave to cool.

4 Spread out each spring roll wrapper and place about 2 tablespoonfuls of the mixture onto one side of each wrapper, facing a corner. Fold the corner over the filling, and once again. Fold in the sides, rather like an envelope, and continue to fold to make a cylindrical shape. Seal the edges with a little water.

5 Heat enough oil to deep-fry the spring rolls then deep-fry them for 5 minutes until golden brown; you may have to fry them in batches. Drain on kitchen paper before serving.

CHEF'S TIP: Spring roll fillings should be as dry as possible since the rolls may burst during frying if the mixture contains too much water.

PO PIA JAY
VEGETARIAN SPRING ROLL

The type of vegetables used in the spring roll filling is a matter of individual taste, but stick to those that remain crisp and firm when cooked. Serve with chilli sauce.

MAKES 5

30g (1/4 cup) carrot
60g (1 1/2 cup) Chinese cabbage
60g (1/2 cup) leek, white part only
30g (1/4 cup) rice vermicelli, soaked until soft
2 tbsp vegetable oil, plus extra for deep-frying
60g (2 1/2 oz) firm tofu, drained
2 tbsp crushed roasted peanuts
5 sheets spring roll wrappers, each about 18cm (7in) square

SEASONINGS:
1 tbsp garlic purée
2 tbsp fish sauce
1 tsp freshly ground black pepper

PLA MUK TOD
FRIED SQUID WITH GARLIC

The term "local dish" usually refers to a recipe that is home-cooked using local ingredients, and one that is not ubiquitous in restaurants. It is essentially a simple and rustic dish such as this recipe.

SERVES 4
500g (18oz) fresh squid, gutted and cleaned
1 small onion
2 tbsp vegetable oil
2 tbsp chopped garlic
1 tsp crushed black peppercorns
1 tbsp oyster sauce
1 tbsp fish sauce
fresh Thai sweet basil and green peppercorns, to garnish

1 Cut the squid into 5cm (2in) pieces. With a sharp knife, lightly score a criss-cross pattern on each piece of squid so when cooked, they curl in a pretty way.

2 Thinly slice the onion. Heat the oil in a wok or frying pan and stir-fry the garlic for 1 minute until light brown, taking care it doesn't burn. Add the onion and stir-fry for 1 minute.

3 Add the peppercorns, squid, oyster sauce and fish sauce and stir-fry vigorously for 2 minutes. Serve garnished with basil leaves and green peppercorns.

CHEF'S TIP: If you can get hold of fresh green peppercorns from Thai supermarkets, they give the dish an authentic peppery fillip.

GAI HOR BAI TOEI
SPICED CHICKEN IN TOEI LEAVES

Toei leaves are known as *pandan* leaves elsewhere in tropical Asia and the botanical name is *screwpine* leaf (see page 9). They are available fresh in most Chinese and Thai supermarkets and their fragrance is faintly reminiscent of vanilla. They also yield a rich, jade green juice when ground.

MAKES 15
500g (18oz) skinless chicken breasts
2 tbsp Yellow Curry Paste (see page 62)
2 tbsp fish sauce
1 tbsp lime juice
1 tsp sugar
about 8 toei leaves
corn or vegetable oil, for deep-frying

1 Cut the chicken into 15 x 4cm (6 x 11$\frac{1}{2}$in) cubes. Mix together the curry paste, fish sauce, lime juice and sugar in a shallow dish, add the chicken and turn until coated in the marinade. Cover the dish, refrigerate and marinate for 30 minutes.

2 Cut or trim each toei leaf into 15 x 15cm long x 4cm wide (15 x 6in long x 1$\frac{1}{2}$in wide) strips. Wrap a toei leaf around each piece of chicken, overlapping once. Tuck in the end firmly to make a triangular shape and secure with a toothpick. Trim off any excess leaf.

3 Heat enough oil in a wok or saucepan to deep-fry the chicken parcels. Fry the chicken in batches for 5–6 minutes. Remove the chicken parcels using a slotted spoon and drain on kitchen paper.

4 Serve the chicken parcels in their leafy wrapper, allowing diners to unwrap them or remove the leaf and arrange on a serving plate.

illustrated on page 7

Fried squid with garlic

KHANOM JEEB

MINCED PORK DUMPLINGS

This takes a liberal leaf from Thailand's Chinese heritage – a fair number of the Thai population are of Chinese descent – and echoes the traditional dim sum dumpling called *shao mai*.

MAKES 16

200g (7oz) minced chicken

100g (4oz) raw prawns (shrimp), minced

40g (1$^{1}/_{2}$oz) water chestnuts, chopped

1 tbsp chopped spring onions (scallions)

2 tsp cornflour (cornstarch)

$^{1}/_{2}$ tsp freshly ground black pepper

1 tbsp fish sauce

1 tbsp sesame oil

16 won ton skins

16 garden peas

1 Blend together all the ingredients, except the won ton skins and peas, in a food processor until a coarse paste. Cook a little nugget in boiling water to taste and adjust the seasoning if necessary.

2 Place 1 heaped teaspoonful of the mixture in the centre of each won ton skin, wet the edges of the won ton and gather up the sides. Squeeze together, leaving the top open. Trim off any excess and pat each parcel firmly to form a flat base and an upright, open dumpling. Top each won ton with a pea.

3 Place the won ton in a steamer and steam for 12 minutes – you may have to cook them in batches. Serve with the Chilli Dipping Sauce (see page 63).

SERVES 4

2 stalks fresh coriander (cilantro), roots and all
2 tbsp vegetable oil
2 tbsp garlic purée
300g (11oz) minced pork
2 tbsp coarsely ground peanuts
2 tbsp fish sauce
3 tbsp palm sugar
$1/2$ tsp freshly ground black pepper
8 fresh or canned peach halves
$1/2$ iceberg (Webbs) lettuce, shredded, to serve

MA HOR
GALLOPING HORSES

No one knows how this equestrian name came about as the finished dish does not look remotely equine. The accepted hypothesis is that they are so delicious one is apt to literally gallop towards them!

1 Chop the coriander (cilantro) very finely. Pour the oil into a wok or frying pan and add the coriander (cilantro) and garlic and stir-fry over a low heat for 2 minutes. Increase the heat to medium, add the minced pork and stir-fry for 3 minutes until cooked. Turn off the heat.

2 Add the peanuts, fish sauce, palm sugar and pepper and stir until combined; the mixture should be fairly dry.

3 Heap the mixture into each peach half and serve on a bed of lettuce.

CHEF'S TIP: You can also use minced prawns (shrimp) or lobster instead of the pork.

FISH AND SHELLFISH

Given that the extensive Thai coastline, and the mighty Chao Praya river and her tributaries are fecund with fish and assorted crustacea, seafood cooking reaches glorious heights in most Thai kitchens. Simply fried and innocent of all but a touch of lemon grass, spiced up, wrapped in banana leaf, bathed in tamarind or coconut cream, each creation is a scrumptious testament to Thai culinary ingenuity.

STEAMED MUSSELS WITH KRACHAI

I particularly love large pots of steamed mussels and this one is infused with lesser ginger (*krachai,* see page 8) and black pepper. Throw table manners to the wind and dip in with your fingers; it's really the only way to enjoy mussels.

SERVES 4

2kg (4½lb) fresh mussels
2 tbsp fresh coriander (cilantro) roots and stems
4 tbsp vegetable oil
1 tbsp shredded lesser ginger (*krachai,* see page 8) or galangal
1 tbsp crushed garlic
1 tsp freshly ground black pepper
juice of 2 limes
2 tbsp fish sauce
100ml (⅓ cup) Chinese wine or dry sherry
large bunch of Thai sweet basil leaves

1 Scrub the mussels well under cold running water, discarding any broken or open shells. Grind the coriander (cilantro) roots and stems using a pestle and mortar or in a coffee grinder.

2 Heat the oil in a wok or frying pan and stir-fry the lesser ginger and garlic for 1 minute then add the coriander (cilantro). Stir-fry for 1 minute.

3 Place a plate or dish in the bottom of a large steamer. Put the mussels in the steamer and sprinkle the fried ingredients over. Add the black pepper, lime juice, fish sauce and Chinese wine and toss the mussels well. Cover the pan and steam for 6–8 minutes.

4 Transfer the mussels and any juices to a large bowl and discard any unopened shells. Serve the mussels garnished with whole and chopped basil leaves.

CHEF'S TIP: The mussels can also be cooked in a large saucepan instead of a steamer, following the instructions in steps 3 and 4. Cover the pan with a lid and shake it occasionally until the mussels are cooked.

Illustrated on previous pages

MASSAMAN PRAWN (SHRIMP) CURRY

The aromatic blend of herbs and spices along with the "fire" of the fresh chillies, add a delicous pungency to the prawns (shrimp). Serve with Sticky Rice (see page 58).

SERVES 4

2 tbsp vegetable oil, plus extra for deep-frying
16 raw tiger prawns (shrimp), shelled, tail left on and deveined
3 tbsp Massaman Curry Paste (see page 63)
150ml (⅔ cup) coconut milk
2 tsp sugar
4 kaffir lime leaves, finely shredded
1 tbsp fish sauce
Cos (Romaine) lettuce leaves, shredded, and 2 tbsp coconut cream, to serve
fresh Thai sweet basil leaves, to garnish

1 Heat enough oil in a wok or saucepan to deep-fry the prawns. Fry the prawns (shrimp) for 1 minute then drain on kitchen paper and keep warm.

2 Heat 2 tablespoons oil in a clean wok or frying pan and cook the Massaman paste for 2 minutes over a low heat.

3 Add the coconut milk and bring to the boil. Stir in the sugar, kaffir lime leaves and fish sauce and cook for 5 seconds then turn off the heat.

4 Arrange the prawns in a serving dish on a bed of shredded lettuce leaves then pour the sauce over. To serve, drizzle with coconut cream and garnish with fresh basil.

Massaman Prawn Curry

PLA PAU BI MAKRUT
GRILLED FISH WITH LIME LEAVES AND LEMON GRASS

The heady perfume of kaffir lime leaves and lemon grass evoke sharp memories of Thai cuisine. This aromatic dish is a village offering in the best culinary tradition of the Chao Praya river.

1 Wash and pat dry the fish fillets. Mix the garlic, kaffir lime leaves and lemon grass with the lime juice, sugar, fish sauce and oil in a shallow dish.

2 Add the fish and spoon the marinade over until coated. Marinate the fish for 1 hour, turning once or twice. Heat a grill to high and place the fish on a foil-lined rack. Spoon the marinade over the fish and grill for 4–5 minutes. Turn the fillets, spoon some more marinade over the top and grill for a further 4–5 minutes.

3 To make the chilli and lime dipping sauce, grind the chillies and garlic using a pestle and mortar or coffee grinder. Combine the ground chillies and garlic with the lime juice and sugar. Serve with the grilled fish.

SERVES 4

4 trout or mackerel fillets
2 cloves garlic, sliced
8 kaffir lime leaves, shredded
3 stalks lemon grass, 5cm (2in) root end, peeled and finely chopped
1 tbsp lime juice
1 tsp sugar
1 tbsp fish sauce
2 tbsp vegetable oil

CHILLI & LIME DIPPING SAUCE:
2–3 red chillies, chopped
2 cloves garlic, chopped
2 tbsp lime juice
1 tsp sugar

PAD PET PLA DUK
FRIED CURRIED FISH

River fish are a staple of many Thai and Vietnamese villagers and they are almost always catfish, which grow to a huge size. Use trout if catfish is unavailable.

SERVES 4

600g (1¼lb) catfish or trout fillets
2 tbsp vegetable oil, plus extra for deep-frying
1 tbsp Red Curry Paste (see page 62)
150ml (⅔ cup) coconut milk
2 tbsp shredded lesser ginger (*krachai*, see page 8) or galangal
2 tbsp fish sauce
1 tbsp sugar
1 tbsp shredded kaffir lime leaves
1 sliced red chilli and fried sliced garlic, to garnish

1 Wash and pat dry the fish fillets and cut in half crossways. Heat enough oil in a wok or saucepan to deep-fry the fish. Fry the fish in batches for 8–10 minutes until the skin is crisp then drain on kitchen paper and set aside.

2 In a clean wok or pan, heat 2 tablespoons oil and fry the red curry paste over a low heat for 2 minutes, stirring. Add the coconut milk, lesser ginger, fish sauce, sugar and kaffir lime leaves and stir for 1 minute.

3 Add the fried fish, spoon the sauce over, and heat through briefly. Garnish with sliced chillies and fried garlic.

GAENG KIEW WAN TALAY
SEAFOOD GREEN CURRY

Green curry is a Thai classic and is unique in that it uses only fresh herbs and spices, rather than dried (although some versions like those from Chiang Mai are an exception to the rule). When cooked with seafood, the results are positively ambrosial.

SERVES 4

2 tbsp Green Curry Paste (see page 62)
400ml (1⅔ cups) coconut milk
4 Thai apple aubergines (eggplant), halved or quartered, or
1 purple aubergine (eggplant), diced into 1cm (½in) cubes
2 tbsp fish sauce
2 tbsp lime juice
small bunch of fresh Thai sweet basil leaves
1 tsp palm sugar
300g (11oz) shelled raw prawns (shrimp)
200g (7oz) squid rings
2 tbsp fried shallots, to garnish

1 Mix together the green curry paste and the coconut milk in a saucepan and bring to the boil.

2 Add the aubergines (eggplant), fish sauce, lime juice, basil leaves and palm sugar and simmer for 5–6 minutes. Add the prawns (shrimp) and squid and simmer for another 2–3 minutes or until the prawns are cooked.

3 Garnish with the fried shallots.

CHEF'S TIP: Thai aubergines (eggplant) come in a plethora of sizes, from large, foot-long specimens to pea-sized ones. The traditional type is the apple aubergine (eggplant) and each one is about the size of a walnut.

illustrated on page 2

Fried Curried Fish

MEAT AND POULTRY

While Thai cooking rests heavily on spice blends, there are many meat and poultry dishes that sit on the side of subtlety. But it is the alchemy between spices and chicken, duck, pork and beef that ultimately seduces. Touched with coconut; perfumed with basil, and lime leaves; curried with chillies and cumin — these dishes have few peers.

CHICKEN AND LEMON GRASS CURRY

In the tradition of yellow curries, this dish is highly aromatic thanks to the addition of lemon grass, basil and kaffir lime leaves. It's also extremely easy to prepare.

SERVES 4

2 skinless chicken breasts, about 250g (9oz) total weight
2 tbsp vegetable oil
2 stalks lemon grass, peeled
1 large onion
400ml (1²/₃ cups) coconut milk
2 tbsp tamarind paste
1 tbsp palm sugar
2 tbsp Yellow Curry Paste (see page 62)
3 kaffir lime leaves (1 leaf, shredded)

1 Cut the chicken into bite-sized pieces, discarding any fatty skin and gristle.

2 Heat half of the the oil in a wok or frying pan and sauté the chicken over a high heat for 3 minutes until golden. Drain on kitchen paper and set aside.

3 Thinly slice the lemon grass and onion. Heat the remaining oil and stir-fry the lemon grass and onion for 2 minutes.

4 Stir in the coconut milk, tamarind paste, palm sugar, yellow curry paste and kaffir lime leaves then simmer for 5 minutes. Return the fried chicken to the wok and simmer for about 10 minutes until reduced and thickened.

CHEF'S TIP: Sautéing the chicken first is a traditional cooking method but you can omit this step with only marginal difference to the taste. Simply add the chicken in step 3 and cook for 3 minutes.

Illustrated on previous pages

CORIANDER AND GARLIC MARINATED CHICKEN

This is a signature dish of many Thai restaurants but there are numerous regional variations. The Thai penchant for using fresh coriander (cilantro), roots and all, is simple culinary ingenuity.

SERVES 4

4 chicken legs on the bone
4 cloves garlic, peeled
2 tbsp fresh coriander (cilantro), roots and all
1 tbsp fish sauce
2 tbsp lime juice
1 tbsp palm sugar
1 tsp freshly ground black pepper
diced cucumber and mango, to serve

1 Make deep slits along the thickest part of each chicken leg.

2 Pound the garlic and coriander using a pestle and mortar until finely minced and mix with the fish sauce, lime juice, palm sugar and pepper.

3 Put the chicken in a shallow dish and pour the marinade over. Marinate the chicken for at least 30 minutes.

4 For best results, barbecue the chicken for about 20–30 minutes, turning occasionally, until cooked through. Alternatively, put the chicken on a rack and cook under a medium grill for about 20–25 minutes, turning once or twice and basting occasionally with a little of the marinade, until cooked through.

5 Serve the chicken with the diced cucumber and mango.

Coriander and Garlic Marinated Chicken

LAP PED KHAO NIEW
ROAST DUCK

Vermilion-rich roast duck is very much a Cantonese speciality, yet Thai cuisine draws from its Chinese heritage to create its own version. A new synergy is forged when the duck is served with Sticky Rice (see page 58), a staple of northern and rural Thailand.

1 To get the best results, hang the duck overnight in a cool, dry place. On the day of cooking, put the duck in a large saucepan, cover with water and bring to the boil. Cook the duck for 6 minutes. (This reduces the amount of fat and gives the skin a nice sheen.)

2 Preheat the oven to 200°C (400°F). Mix together the ingredients for the marinade. Rub the marinade all over the duck and set aside for 10 minutes.

3 Place the duck on a rack in a roasting pan and roast for 1$\frac{1}{2}$–2 hours. To test if the duck is cooked, pierce the thickest part of the duck with a metal skewer and if the juices run clear, it is ready. Allow the duck to rest for 30 minutes before carving.

4 Serve with sticky rice, pink pickled ginger and chilli dipping sauce.

SERVES 6–8
1 oven-ready duckling, about 2.5kg (5$\frac{1}{2}$lb)
pink pickled ginger and Dried Shrimp, Chilli, Lime Juice & Basil dip (see page 63), to serve

MARINADE
2 tbsp hoisin sauce
2 tbsp Chinese wine or dry sherry
1 tbsp clear honey
pinch cochineal food colouring (optional)

YAM MAKUA YAO
AUBERGINE AND MINCED PORK

A local staple in many parts of southern Thailand, the minced pork with chunks of Thai aubergine (eggplant) is delicious served with curry and Jasmine rice.

SERVES 4

250g (9oz) purple aubergine (eggplant)
2 tbsp dried shrimps
1 tbsp vegetable oil
2 cloves garlic, crushed
1/2 tsp freshly ground black pepper
150g (5oz) minced pork
1 tbsp fish sauce
1 tbsp palm sugar
2 tbsp sliced shallots
juice of 1 lime
5 red or green chillies, deseeded and sliced
fresh coriander (cilantro), to garnish

1 Preheat the grill to high. Halve the aubergine (eggplant) lengthways and grill for 8 minutes, skin-side up until the skin is charred. Leave to cool slightly then peel the skin off and cut the aubergine (eggplant) into small dice. Set aside.

2 Soak the dried shrimps in hot water for 15 minutes until softened. Drain and pound using a pestle and mortar until finely ground then set aside.

3 Heat the oil in a wok or frying pan and fry the garlic and pepper for 1 minute then add the minced pork and fish sauce. Continue to cook over a low heat until the pork is well done, about 8 minutes. Add the palm sugar, shallots, lime juice and chillies and mix well.

4 Add the aubergine (eggplant) and ground shrimps to the wok and stir-fry over a low heat for 1 minute. Serve garnished with fresh coriander (cilantro).

CHEF'S TIP: Courgettes (zucchini) cooked this way are also delicious.

NUA SARB NORMAI
MINCED BEEF WITH BAMBOO SHOOTS

This hearty dish reflects Thailand's close proximity to Vietnam and China, and is a compendium of flavours that draws from all three countries.

SERVES 4

2 tbsp sesame oil
3 garlic cloves, crushed
200g (7oz) minced chuck or sirloin beef
100g (4oz) canned ready-sliced bamboo shoots, drained
60g (21/2oz) canned water chestnuts, drained
1 tsp chilli powder
1 tbsp fish sauce
1 tsp sugar
2 tbsp chopped fresh coriander (cilantro), to garnish

1 Heat the sesame oil in a wok or frying pan and stir-fry the garlic for 1 minute until light golden. Add the beef and stir-fry for 2 minutes until browned.

2 Add the remaining ingredients and stir-fry vigorously for 2 minutes. Sprinkle a little water over the beef if the mixture becomes too dry.

3 Garnish the mince with fresh coriander (cilantro).

Aubergine and Minced Pork

PANAENG NUA
PENANG DRY BEEF CURRY

Southern Thai cooking draws liberally from Indian and Malaysian influences; the latter is also a hybrid that goes back centuries. The term "*Paneang*" has become generic within the realm of Thai curries, and refers to the neighbouring Malaysian island of Penang. Serve the curry with rice noodles.

1 In a dry wok or frying pan, fry the coriander and cumin powder over a low heat until the fragrance exudes. Remove and mix with the red curry paste and garlic purée.

2 Return the paste mixture to the wok and add the coconut milk, stir well, and simmer for 5 minutes.

3 Cut the beef into chunks and add to the wok. Cook for 5 minutes, stirring well. Reduce the heat and simmer for 10 minutes until a faint trace of reddish oil rises to the surface of the curry.

4 Add the fish sauce, palm sugar, kaffir lime leaves and lime juice then cook for a further 3 minutes.

CHEF'S TIP: This is a moderately spiced curry but you can increase the amount of red curry paste if you prefer more heat and spice.

SERVES 4
2 tbsp ground coriander
2 tsp ground cumin
$1\frac{1}{2}$ tbsp Red Curry Paste (see page 62)
$1\frac{1}{2}$ tbsp garlic purée
300ml ($1\frac{1}{4}$ cups) coconut milk
450g (1lb) sirloin or rump beef
2 tbsp fish sauce
3 tbsp palm sugar
6 kaffir lime leaves
2 tbsp lime juice
lime wedges, to serve

VEGETABLE DISHES

The soul of Thai cooking lies in the rustic heart of the country and even though the cuisine has become a sophisticated global phenomenon, simply cooked vegetables are still held in reverence. The range from nature's earthy bounty is a veritable rainbow spectrum — aubergines (eggplant) of every hue, leafy greens of every imaginable taste, gourds, marrows and even fruits end up in gustatory splendour.

GAI YAD SAI
SAVOURY STUFFED OMELETTE

The simplicity of this dish belies its rich culinary heritage, albeit of rural Thailand. Mixed vegetables, mushrooms (and sometimes meat) are stir-fried then encased in an omelette.

SERVES 4

6 dried Chinese mushrooms
100g (4oz) fresh tofu, drained
4 tbsp vegetable oil
1 tbsp chopped garlic
2 tbsp finely chopped spring onions (scallions)
75g (scant 1 cup) garden peas
2 tbsp fish sauce
1/2 tsp freshly ground black pepper
5 eggs, lightly beaten
few sprigs of fresh coriander (cilantro) and 1 red chilli, sliced, to garnish

1 Soak the mushrooms in hot water until softened then remove the hard stalks and slice the caps. Pat dry the tofu using kitchen towels and mash with a fork.

2 Heat half the oil in a wok or frying pan and stir-fry the garlic until light brown. Add the sliced mushrooms and stir-fry for 1 minute. Add the tofu and continue to stir-fry for 2 minutes. Next, add the spring onions (scallions), peas, fish sauce and black pepper, stir, then remove from the heat.

3 Heat the remaining oil in a large frying pan and pour in the egg. Turn the pan until the egg coats the base and cook over a medium heat, swirling as you do so to make an omelette.

4 When nearly cooked – the centre should still be soft – heap the cooked ingredients in the centre and the flip the omelette over to make a half moon shape. Cook for 3–4 minutes until the edges are crisp.

5 Remove the omelette from the pan and serve garnished with fresh coriander (cilantro) and sliced chillies.

Illustrated on previous pages

PHAD TENDER STEM BROCCOLI
TENDER STEM BROCCOLI WITH OYSTER SAUCE AND MUSHROOMS

This Chinese-influenced dish is traditionally made using the popular Chinese vegetable, *kai lan*, although tender stem broccoli makes an excellent alternative and comes closest in flavour.

SERVES 4

300g (11oz) tender stem broccoli
6 fresh field mushrooms, stalks trimmed
2 tbsp vegetable oil
1 tbsp chopped garlic
1 tbsp shredded ginger
2 tbsp Chinese wine or dry sherry
2 tbsp oyster sauce
1/2 tsp freshly ground black pepper
2 tbsp water

1 Cut the broccoli into 5cm (2in) lengths, wash and drain.

2 Heat the oil in a wok or frying pan and stir-fry the garlic and ginger for 1 minute. Toss in the broccoli and mushrooms and stir-fry over a high heat for 1 minute.

3 Add the wine, oyster sauce, black pepper and water and continue to stir-fry for 2 minutes. Serve immediately.

CHEF'S TIP: To keep the broccoli crisp and retain its colour, blanch it first in boiling water for 30 seconds, drain and refresh under cold running water before stir-frying.

Tender Stem Broccoli with Oyster Sauce and Mushrooms

GAENG NOPAKKAO
MIXED VEGETABLE CURRY

Courtesy of my good friend and Thai chef supremo, Tym Srisawatt, who has won many awards for her vegetarian dishes, *gaeng nopakkao* is a most welcome vegetarian dish after a surfeit of meat. Serve with Sticky Rice (see page 58).

SERVES 4

150g (5oz) Savoy or green cabbage
1 carrot
4 Thai apple aubergines (eggplant), each the size of a large walnut
2 tbsp vegetable oil
2 tbsp Yellow Curry Paste (see page 62)
250ml (1 cup) coconut milk
1 tbsp fish sauce
1 tbsp palm sugar
3 tbsp coconut cream, to serve (optional)

1 Roughly chop the Savoy cabbage, thickly slice the carrot and quarter the aubergines (eggplant). Wash and pat dry the vegetables.

2 Heat the oil in a wok or frying pan and stir-fry the yellow curry paste for 1 minute. Add the coconut milk and bring to the boil.

3 Add all the vegetables, fish sauce and palm sugar. Reduce the heat and simmer for 8 minutes, stirring occasionally until the vegetables are tender. Drizzle the coconut cream over, if using.

PHAD PAK RUAM
STIR-FRIED MIXED VEGETABLES

This is a real jewel of a dish: a crunchy, spicy compendium of different vegetables in a peppery sauce. This recipe can be adapted to suit almost any combination of vegetables.

SERVES 4

90g (3½oz) tender stem broccoli or *kai lan*
90g (3½oz) cauliflower florets
1 carrot
10 fresh field mushrooms
12 mange tout (snow peas)
3 tbsp vegetable oil
1 tbsp crushed garlic
1 tbsp sesame oil
1 tbsp fish sauce
1 tbsp oyster sauce
½ tsp freshly ground black pepper
½ tsp sugar

1 Cut the broccoli and cauliflower into bite-sized pieces. Slice the carrot into rounds and halve the mushrooms.

2 Bring a large saucepan of water to the boil and blanch all the vegetables for 1 minute then drain well and refresh under cold running water.

3 Heat the oil in a wok or frying pan and stir-fry the garlic until light brown. Add all the vegetables and stir-fry over a high heat for 1 minute.

4 Add the sesame oil, fish sauce, oyster sauce, pepper and sugar and stir-fry for a further 30 seconds until combined. Serve immediately.

CHEF'S TIP: If the vegetables are blanched before stir-frying, there is no need to add extra water.

1 Slice the stalks of the morning glory into 5cm (2in) pieces and shred the leaves roughly. Wash and drain thoroughly.

2 Heat the oil in a wok and stir-fry the garlic for 1 minute until light brown then add the curry paste and sugar. Fry for another minute then add the morning glory and water.

3 Cover the wok and cook over a high heat until the morning glory is tender, about 3 minutes.

PHAAD PAK BUNG
STIR FRIED MORNING GLORY

Morning glory is a vegetable indigenous to most of Southeast Asia, and in Thailand it grows vigorously. Also known as *water convolvulus* and *water spinach*, it is rich in nutrients and crisp and crunchy when stir-fried. Spinach makes a decent substitute.

SERVES 4

200g (7oz) morning glory
2 tbsp vegetable oil
2 cloves garlic, sliced
1 tbsp Red or Yellow Curry Paste (see page 62)
1 tsp sugar
100ml ($1/3$ cup) water

NOODLES AND RICE

It may have been the Chinese who introduced noodles to Thailand but the country is not known as Asia's rice bowl for nothing. Steamed, fluffy Jasmine rice or sticky rice are at the very heart of a Thai meal and make the most perfect foil for spicy dishes. Noodles turn up in myriad guises, often enriched with chicken, shrimp, squid and inevitably, spices.

MEE KROB
CRISPY NOODLES

Practically a national dish in Thailand, where each village or region has its own variation, this recipe comes from Bangkok and typifies the cooking of the south.

SERVES 4

vegetable oil, for deep-frying
300g (3 cups) dried rice vermicelli
2 tbsp chopped garlic
150g (5oz) white crab meat
250g (9oz) peeled raw prawns (shrimp)
3 spring onions (scallions), cut into thin 5cm (2in) lengths
2 tbsp chilli paste
2 tbsp fish sauce
2 tbsp lime juice
1 tsp sugar
200g (scant 1 cup) beansprouts

1 Heat enough oil in a large wok or saucepan to deep-fry the vermicelli then fry a few handfuls at a time until they puff up and turn a pale golden colour. When cooked, drain on kitchen paper and set aside.

2 Pour off all but 2 tablespoons of the oil and fry the garlic until light brown. Add the crab meat, prawns (shrimp) and spring onions (scallions) and stir-fry for 2 minutes.

3 Add the chilli paste, fish sauce, lime juice and sugar then stir. Add the crisp vermicelli and toss gently. Turn off the heat and toss in the beansprouts (they should be practically raw).

Illustrated on previous pages

KHAO SOY
CHICKEN CURRY NOODLES

This hails from Chiang Mai and reflects the cuisine of Burma, Thailand's north western neighbour. It is also used as the template for many Malaysian and Singaporean spicy noodle dishes. In the north, it is usually served with a garnish of salted vegetables but this is an acquired taste.

SERVES 4

450g (1lb) skinless chicken breasts
400g (5 cups) fresh egg noodles
2 tbsp vegetable oil
2 cloves garlic, crushed
2 tbsp Red Curry Paste (see page 62)
1 litre (4 cups) coconut milk
2 tbsp fish sauce
1 chicken stock cube, crumbled
2 tbsp lime juice
1 tsp sugar
fried shallots and fresh coriander (cilantro), to garnish

1 Slice the chicken into strips. Blanch the noodles in boiling water for 1 minute then drain.

2 Heat the oil in a wok or frying pan and stir-fry the garlic for 1 minute until light brown. Add the curry paste and stir-fry for 2 minutes over a low heat.

3 Add the coconut milk, fish sauce, stock cube, lime juice and sugar, stir well, and bring to the boil. Reduce the heat, add the chicken and simmer over a medium heat for 10 minutes, stirring occasionally.

4 To serve, divide the noodles between four bowls and top with the chicken curry. Garnish with the shallots and coriander (cilantro).

Chicken Curry Noodles

RICE NOODLES WITH CHICKEN

Simple Thai street food, *phad Thai* is ubiquitous throughout the country.
A sprinkling of chopped or ground peanuts is a typically Thai garnish.

1 Thinly slice the chicken breast.

2 Heat the oil in a wok or frying pan and stir-fry the garlic for
1 minute until light brown. Add the chicken and stir-fry over a
high heat for 3 minutes until the chicken is golden.

3 Add the beansprouts, noodles, fish sauce, soy sauce, lime
juice and chilli powder and stir-fry for 2 minutes.

4 Pour in the water and continue to stir-fry for another 2
minutes. Serve garnished with the chopped peanuts and basil.

SERVES 4
250g (9oz) skinless chicken breast
3 tbsp vegetable oil
2 tbsp chopped garlic
200g (scant 1 cup) beansprouts
300g (4 cups) fresh rice noodles
2 tbsp fish sauce
2 tbsp dark soy sauce
1 tbsp lime juice
1 tsp chilli powder
3 tbsp water
3 tbsp chopped peanuts and fresh Thai sweet
basil, to garnish

PHAD SIEW
FRIED RICE NOODLES WITH DARK SOY SAUCE

Given Thailand's close ties with China, both historically and geographically, noodles form an integral part of most meals. Rice noodles come either fresh or dried. Fresh noodles simply need heating through.

1 Heat the oil in a wok or frying pan and stir-fry the garlic for 1 minute. Add the prawns (shrimp) and stir-fry over a high heat for 2 minutes.

2 Briefly rinse the fresh rice noodles under a hot running tap to remove the oil that usually coats them.

3 Add the rice noodles, beansprouts and all the seasonings to the wok and stir-fry for 2 minutes. Pour in the water and continue to stir-fry vigorously for 2 minutes.

4 Garnish with a wedge of lime and serve accompanied by the garlic and chilli sauce.

CHEF'S TIP: Prawns (shrimp) can be substituted with chicken, pork or mushrooms as a vegetarian option.

SERVES 4

3 tbsp vegetable oil
2 tbsp chopped garlic
250g (9oz) medium peeled raw prawns (shrimp)
300g (4 cups) fresh rice noodles
100g (scant $\frac{1}{2}$ cup) beansprouts
2 tbsp dark soy sauce
2 tbsp oyster sauce
1 tbsp sesame oil
1 tsp freshly ground black pepper
4 tbsp water
wedges of lime, to garnish
garlic & chilli sauce, to serve

KHAO NIEW
STICKY RICE

Otherwise known as glutinous rice in some Southeast Asian countries, this staple is traditionally served at every meal and goes particularly well with curries. For the best results, soak the rice for several hours, or even overnight, before steaming.

SERVES 4
300g (1¹/₂ cups) glutinous (sticky) rice
¹/₂ tsp salt

1 Put the soaked rice in a large bowl with the salt. Cover with cold water, so that it covers the rice by about 2.5cm (1in).

2 After several hours, the rice will have soaked up most of the water. Drain then transfer to a steamer. Steam the rice for 25 minutes until tender.

KHAO PHAD
PINEAPPLE RICE

Here, fried rice is studded with seafood, chillies and spices. It cuts a real dash when served in a scooped-out pineapple half, a real pièce de résistance. It is believed to have originated in the Thai royal kitchens.

SERVES 4
1 fresh pineapple, about 2.5kg (5¹/₂lb)
3 tbsp vegetable oil
2 tbsp chopped garlic
2 tbsp sliced shallots
3 eggs
200g (7oz) shelled raw prawns (shrimp)
450g (6 cups) cold, cooked long-grain rice
2 tbsp fish sauce
2 red chillies, sliced
2 tbsp chopped spring onions (scallions)
1 vegetable stock cube, crumbled

1 Halve the pineapple lengthways. Scoop out the pineapple flesh, leaving a border about 1cm (¹/₂in) thick. Remove the tough core and finely dice the pineapple.

2 Heat the oil in a wok or frying pan and stir-fry the garlic and shallots for 2 minutes. Push to one side and crack the eggs into the wok and cook, stirring until scrambled.

3 Add the prawns (shrimp) and stir-fry for 2 minutes. Add 3 tablespoons of the chopped pineapple (reserving the rest for another use), the cold rice, fish sauce, chillies, spring onions (scallions) and stock cube and stir-fry over a high heat for 3 minutes until the rice is thoroughly heated through.

4 Spoon the rice into the pineapple shell before serving.

PASTES AND DIPS

Most curries rely on a blend of herbs and spices as a base and these pastes are often family recipes handed down the generations. Dips are an integral part of every Thai meal and are usually an ingenious blend of aromatics like lemon grass, garlic, galangal, ginger, kaffir lime leaves and basil that work in harmony with the chilli and dried spices.

Chilli Dipping Sauce

Shrimp Paste with Lime Leaf

Dried Shrimp, Chilli, Lime juice & Basil

Muslim Curry Paste

Green Curry Paste

Red Curry Paste

Yellow Curry Paste

CHILLI DIPPING SAUCE
NAM PRIK NUM

This pungent dip is ubiquitous throughout Thailand as a perfect accompaniment for steamed, fried and grilled foods.

MAKES APPROXIMATELY 200G (7OZ)
OF SAUCE
15 large green chillies, stalks removed
6 cloves garlic
9 shallots, peeled
$1/2$ tsp shrimp paste
$1/2$ tsp salt
1 tbsp fish sauce
3 tbsp lime juice
1 tsp sugar

1 Dry-fry the chillies in a frying pan over a low heat for about 5 minutes, turning occasionally, until slightly blackened. Remove from the pan and repeat with the garlic and shallots for 5 minutes until slightly seared and blackened.

2 Grind the chillies using a pestle and mortar or a coffee grinder until they are crushed. Next, add the garlic and continue to grind.

3 Add the shallots and grind again followed by the shrimp paste and salt. Grind until the ingredients form a fairly smooth paste. Stir in the fish sauce, lime juice and sugar.

4 Transfer to a bowl and chill, covered, until ready to serve.

DRIED SHRIMP, CHILLI, LIME JUICE & BASIL
NAM PRIK HORAPA

This is a versatile condiment that can be used as a dipping sauce or as a spice paste for fried poultry, meat and fish.

MAKES APPROXIMATELY 200G (7OZ) OF
SAUCE
3 tbsp dried shrimps
120ml ($1/2$ cup) hot water
4 red chillies
juice of 3 limes
2 tsp sugar
1 tsp fish sauce
1 tsp finely chopped sweet basil
2 tbsp water

1 Soak the dried shrimps in the hot water until softened then drain thoroughly.

2 Grind the shrimps using a pestle and mortar or a coffee grinder until finely ground then add the chillies. Continue to grind until mixed together.

3 Mix the lime juice with the sugar, fish sauce and chopped basil. Combine with the ground ingredients and add the water.

4 Transfer to a bowl and chill, covered, until ready to serve.

SHRIMP PASTE WITH LIME LEAF
NAM PRIK KAPI

A zesty dip for fried seafood, or it can be mixed with warm, cooked rice as a quick savoury dish. The traditional dip does not contain lime leaves but they do add a delicious fragrant tang.

MAKES APPROXIMATELY 150G (5OZ)
OF SAUCE
1 piece shrimp paste, about 4 x 4 x 1cm
($1^1/_2$ x $1^1/_2$ x $1/_2$in) thick
6 red chillies
4 kaffir lime leaves, sliced
1 tbsp hot water
pinch of salt
juice of 3 limes

1 Wrap the shrimp paste in foil then toast it over a gas flame for about 3 minutes until slightly charred. The easiest way to do this is to mould the shrimp paste over the tip of a bamboo or metal skewer then toast and turn until done.

2 Grind the chillies using a pestle and mortar or a coffee grinder until finely ground then add the shrimp paste and lime leaves. Continue until a thick paste then stir in the hot water, salt and lime juice.

4 Transfer to a bowl and chill, covered, until ready to serve.

CHEF'S TIP: The shrimp paste can also be wrapped in foil and grilled, turning halfway, for 8 minutes.

MUSLIM CURRY PASTE
NAM PRIK MASSAMAN

This hails from southern Thailand where many Thai Muslims live, and has evolved from a mix of Thai-Malaysian origins.

MAKES APPROXIMATELY 200G (7OZ)
OF PASTE
2 tbsp ground coriander
1 tbsp ground cumin
1 tsp turmeric powder
1 tbsp chilli powder
2 tbsp chopped onions
4 cloves garlic, chopped
4 thin slices galangal, chopped
1 tbsp shrimp paste
120ml ($1/2$ cup) vegetable oil

1 Dry-fry the spices in a frying pan over a low heat for 8 minutes until fragrant.

2 Grind the onions, garlic, galangal and shrimp paste using a pestle and mortar or coffee grinder until fine and creamy in consistency. Mix with the ground spices.

3 Heat the oil in a frying pan and fry the paste over a medium-low heat for 10 minutes, stirring continuously. The paste will absorb most of the oil during frying but when the oil begins to exude, it is ready.

4 Remove from the heat and cool. Transfer to an airtight jar and use as needed, keeping any excess well covered with plastic wrap or a tight lid in the refrigerator.

CHEF'S TIP: 1 tbsp will suffice for 450g (1lb) of meat, poultry or seafood.

YELLOW CURRY PASTE
NAM PRIK GAENG LIANG

Less well known than red or green curry, this paste has close ties with Malaysian and Burmese curries in its use of turmeric.

MAKES APPROXIMATELY 220G (8OZ)
OF PASTE
6 dried chillies
2 tbsp ground coriander
1 tsp ground cumin
1 tbsp shrimp paste
50g fresh turmeric or 1 tsp turmeric powder
1 large onion, sliced
4 cloves garlic, chopped
2 stalks lemon grass, peeled and roughly chopped
1 tbsp chopped galangal
1 tsp salt
120ml ($^1/_2$ cup) vegetable oil

1 Soak the dried chillies in hot water until softened then drain and slice. Dry-fry the coriander and cumin in a frying pan over a low heat for 8 minutes until fragrant.

2 Grind all other ingredients, except the salt and oil, as you would for the green curry paste until fine and creamy in consistency. Mix with the ground spices and salt.

3 Heat the oil in a frying pan and fry the paste over a medium-low heat for 10 minutes, stirring continuously. The paste will absorb most of the oil during frying but when the oil begins to exude, it is ready.

4 Remove from the heat and leave to cool. Transfer to an airtight jar and use as needed, keeping any excess well covered with plastic wrap or a tight lid in the refrigerator.

CHEF'S TIP: 1 tbsp will suffice for 450g (1lb) of meat, poultry or seafood.

GREEN CURRY PASTE
NAM PRIK GAENG KHIAW WAN

Thai green curry is practically a national dish, winning fans across the world with its aromatic blend of herbs and spices that marry well with meat, chicken and seafood.

MAKES APPROXIMATELY 200G (7OZ)
OF PASTE
2 stalks lemon grass, peeled and roughly chopped
2 slices galangal, about 5mm ($^1/_4$in) thick, chopped
4 green chillies, roughly chopped
1 tsp black peppercorns
3 tbsp chopped fresh coriander (cilantro) roots, stalks and leaves
1 tbsp shrimp paste
3 lime leaves
2 tbsp chopped onions
4 cloves garlic, chopped
120ml ($^1/_2$) cup vegetable oil

1 Grind the lemon grass, galangal, chillies and coriander using a pestle and mortar or coffee grinder. Gradually add the other ingredients, except the oil, a little at a time so as not to overcrowd the mortar or grinder. Grind until a fine, almost creamy paste.

2 Heat the oil in a frying pan and fry the paste over a medium-low heat for 10 minutes, stirring continuously. The paste will absorb most of the oil during frying but when the oil begins to exude, it is ready.

3 Remove from the heat and leave to cool. Transfer to an airtight jar and use as needed, keeping any excess well covered, with plastic wrap or a tight lid in the refrigerator.

CHEF'S TIP: 1 tbsp will suffice for 450g (1lb) of meat, poultry or seafood.

RED CURRY PASTE
NAM PRIK GAENG DAENG

This spice paste is the base for what is probably one of the most well-known Thai curries. It's versatile and lends itself to meat, seafood and vegetables alike.

MAKES APPROXIMATELY 220G (8OZ)
OF PASTE
10 dried chillies
2 tbsp ground coriander
1 tsp ground cumin
1 tsp black peppercorns
1 onion, sliced
2 stalks lemon grass, peeled and chopped
1 tbsp chopped galangal
4 cloves garlic, chopped
4 kaffir lime leaves, sliced
1 tbsp shrimp paste
1 tsp salt
120ml ($^1/_2$ cup) vegetable oil

1 Soak the dried chillies in hot water until softened then drain and slice. Meanwhile, dry-fry the coriander and cumin in a frying pan over a medium-low heat for about 8 minutes until fragrant.

2 Grind the peppercorns, chillies, onion, lemon grass and galangal using a pestle and mortar or coffee grinder. Add the garlic, kaffir lime leaves and shrimp paste, a little at a time so as not to overcrowd the mortar or grinder. Grind until a fine, almost creamy paste. Mix the paste with the shrimp paste, toasted spices and salt.

3 Heat the oil in a frying pan and fry the paste over a low heat for 10 minutes, stirring constantly. The paste will absorb most of the oil during frying but when the oil begins to exude, it is ready

4 Remove from the heat and leave to cool. Transfer to an airtight jar and use as needed, keeping any excess well covered with plastic wrap or a tight lid in the refrigerator.

CHEF'S TIP: 1 tbsp of paste will suffice for 450g (1lb) of meat, poultry or seafood.

ACKNOWLEGEMENTS

My love for Thai food and the cultural semantics knows no bounds and when Jacqui Small commissioned me to write this book, it was delicious grist to the Thai culinary mill. I would like to thank Nicola Graimes for her meticulous work in editing my text and leaving no stone unturned to eliminate any culinary ambiguity. My utmost thanks to Peter Cassidy for his genius in giving my food such stunning dimensions, to Ashley Western for his unflagging passion in the task of brilliant conceptualizing, to Tym Srisawatt, my dearest Thai restaurateur friend who has enhanced and enriched my knowledge of Thai cuisine no end, and last but not least, to Pom, my trusty kitchen assistant for all her help.